Don't Give Up on Your Kids

Understanding and Believing in Teens

S. J. CARR

iUniverse, Inc.
New York   Bloomington

Copyright © 2010 by S. J. Carr

iUniverse books may be ordered through booksellers or by contacting:

iUniverse
1663 Liberty Drive
Bloomington, IN 47403
www.iuniverse.com
1-800-Authors (1-800-288-4677)

ISBN: 978-1-4502-6847-9 (sc)
ISBN: 978-1-4502-6848-6 (ebook)

Printed in the United States of America

iUniverse rev. date: 11/22/2010

"Too often, we underestimate the power of a touch, a smile, a kind word, a listening ear, an honest compliment or the smallest act of caring, all of which have the potential to turn a life around."

– Leo S. Bascaqlia

Dedication

This book is dedicated to John and Betty Carr and my family, without whom I would not be who I am or where I am today.

Forward

Raising teens can be extremely challenging: dealing with peer pressure, school issues and family troubles, not to mention hormones, drugs and alcohol. When things become difficult and behaviour gets out of control, parents are unsure who to talk to and don't know where to turn for help.

I wanted to write a book that parents could relate to, written in terms that parents could understand. Parents want clear, simple and effective strategies that they can use to gain a better understanding of their teens' behaviour, especially when attitudes and defiance begin.

Throughout this book, it may seem as if I am taking the teens' side at times, but this is not the case. Taking sides isn't the answer and doesn't solve the problems. I want both sides to be heard, so that an understanding and solution becomes clear.

As a Child and Youth Worker who works directly with troubled youth, I have come to understand their side and have listened to and helped them process the many issues they face. However, as a parent myself, I also understand the parents' side. I want parents to understand that it is not in any way their fault if they are having problems with their teens or preteens. I am here simply to share some of the observations and techniques that I have learned over the years that have helped me get through to the kids that I have worked with. Teens today do have many different issues to deal with; it can be a very confusing time for them, which is why understanding your teens and building a solid relationship with them is essential.

In order to write a book about understanding teens, I felt that it was important to hear from the teens themselves. Therefore, I have written this book in two parts. Part One is meant to help parents understand where their teens are coming from, how they feel, what kinds of issues they are facing and, most importantly, how to treat and communicate with their teens without creating further arguments.

Part Two contains feedback I have received from teens who have struggled with issues such as parenting, peers, school, drugs and alcohol as well as internal struggles that compromise their self-worth and affect how they see and interact in society. Teens opened up about some of the issues they face and how different issues affect them. They provide some words of advice to parents, teachers and adults in general about how it feels to be mistreated and misunderstood by adults sometimes, how judgements are sometimes made against them just because they are teens.

Instead of putting labels on kids, let's take the time to get to know who they are, what they want from life and how we as adults can assist them on their journey. Above all, teens need support and guidance from parents; they should be able to approach their parents without the fear of being judged. They need to know that parents will be there to support them through anything, the good as well as the bad. Parents and teens alike should understand that it is possible to develop a better relationship, no matter how bad things may be. If you presently have a rocky relationship with your teens, know that it is reversible. Start today to open the lines of communication. Most importantly, don't give up.

In the chapters that follow, you will gain insight into some of the trials and tribulations of raising teens. Keep in mind that there are no experts; every child, every parent and Every case brings differences, there is no right way, it is trial and error to see what strategies work best for your family. My goal is to bridge the gap of communication between youth and their parents. If this book helps just one family open their communication and provides parents with even one idea that they can use, then I will have accomplished my goal.

Contents

Part Two:

Part One

Chapter One

~Misunderstood~

A common complaint from teens is that they feel misunderstood: they feel as if nobody understands where they are coming from. This feeling, however warranted, creates friction between the teen and the parent. The teenage years can be a very difficult time; teenagers feel as if they are grown up but, at the same time, feel confused about what their future holds. They may be going through so many biological changes that they themselves may not know why they feel the way they do. It can be a very trying time for both the parent and the teen.

Conflicts arise between parents and teen when the teens feel that they are grown up and don't need parental guidance anymore. They feel that they can make decisions about their own life. Parents feel that they are trying to help their teens and still need control over their teens' lives. This is where the conflicts begin. The truth is both the teens and the parents are right, which is why the "heated discussions" begin.

Teens are looking for independence while parents don't want to let go of the control.

From the parents' view: Parents sometimes feel that their teens are too irresponsible, immature and impulsive to make informed decisions about their own lives. How can wild and crazy teens make decisions that will affect their future? Parents are afraid that if they allow their teens to make decisions, they will make wrong choices that can affect their future. While these are all potentially true, there comes a point when you have to let go and hope that you have instilled in them the proper values and morals that will enable them to make the right choices. They may not always make the right choices, but after all, life is a learning process.

From the teens' view: Growing up means being grown up. They feel that since they are "not kids anymore", they should be able to make decisions about their own lives and don't want their parents telling them what to do. The more the parents try to "interfere" in their lives, the more they feel they have to pull away.

~Overwhelmed~

As adults, we may think that teens have it made, that they have no real responsibilities. Adults may assume that all teens have to do is get up, go to school, socialize, finish their day at 3:30 and continue to socialize with their friends. Parents may also think that just because teens don't have to worry about paying the mortgage and bills, that they are getting off easy and shouldn't complain.

But teens do have responsibility and feel pressure. Not only do they have to live up to your expectations and schooling, they also have the pressures of fitting in socially within their peer groups. While this may not seem like a big deal to adults, it can be a very challenging and stressful time for teens who are struggling to find themselves. Some teens feel that they don't fit in anywhere. They may be struggling both academically and socially at school, and may also be having problems relating to their parents at home. It doesn't take much for teens to feel overwhelmed.

Overwhelmed feelings can lead to frustration, anger and a total breakdown of communication. They just stop caring. When they stop caring, they can turn to drugs and alcohol to numb the pain.

When teens feel too much pressure and have no one to talk to, they may become unsure of what to do or where to turn and begin to internalize these feelings. Many times, they feel alone and feel as though they are the only ones who are feeling like this. Even if they do have friends they can talk to, they may choose not to, out of the fear of being ridiculed. They may act as if everything is fine, even if they are in turmoil inside.

This is why it is important to know your teens. If you can sense when your teens are having a hard time, then you may be able to validate their feelings and let them know that mixed-up feelings and turmoil can be a normal part of growing up. Let them know that you don't expect them to be perfect; reassure them and accept them as they are.

In order to understand them, we need to try to see things from their point of view. In their eyes, life may not be that easy, and although they may not have the same pressures that adults face, they have different stresses that are equally valid. Be open and honest with them, share stories from your youth, things that you may have gone through. Sometimes it helps to know that they are not the only ones who have ever felt confused.

Overwhelmed with school: When they feel overwhelmed, instead of telling them what to do, help them work through the issues by breaking them down. It is much easier to deal with one issue at a time than to sort out everything at once. By helping them break down their problems into smaller ones, it makes the problem seem much more bearable and provides them with problem-solving skills that they can carry with them throughout their lives. Keep the lines of communication open and do frequent check-ins with them, just touching base. If they are having problems at school, encourage them talk to their teachers instead of avoiding the issue by skipping classes. If teachers are aware that they are having problems, they can work with your teens and help them, without making the teens feel bad or worthless.

If your teens have approached the teachers and nothing is being done, don't give up: have them talk to their guidance counselor or principal. There are many different avenues that school boards can take when teens are having problems.

Classroom settings don't work for everyone. Some teens like to work independently at their own pace while still attaining the credits needed to graduate.

Working independently takes away the classroom pressures of peers knowing how quickly or slowly they work. They don't have to keep up with their peers; they can simply work at their own pace. When working independently, they can remain in the classroom, go into a separate class where there are several kids working independently or, in some cases, they can take independent study booklets home. It really does take away a lot of pressure and makes them feel independent and good about themselves and their future.

Skipping:

Many parents and teachers reading this many not agree with what I am going to say, however I feel it is important to mention as it is a big problem for many parents and teens and leads to many arguments. I'm going to discuss the issue of skipping. Skipping can be part of being a teen, most teens have skipped at some point. The important thing for your teens to realize is that there are differences in skipping.

When my kids started high school, I had a realistic talk with them, I told them that I didn't expect them to never skip a class. What I told them is that *they* are the ones who are responsible for their education and their future. I explained that they may be able to miss the odd class or two and still keep up their grades, but it becomes a problem when too much skipping begins to affect their grades. I explained that by doing this, they are only hurting themselves, since if they fail the class, they will have to redo the class, possibly even adding on a semester after they graduate, thereby extending their school career.

Years ago, that may have not mattered as much to teens, as they could drop out of school and work. Now, the government is beginning to implement strategies to keep teens in school. In Ontario, the government has recently implemented a law that does not allow teens to get their full "G" driving license unless they have graduated. This has become a very big incentive for teens to stay in school and therefore limit or self-regulate their own skipping, as most teens look forward to getting their driver's license. It puts the accountability on them.

Some of you reading this may think I'm saying it's okay for teens to skip classes. Take a minute to think about the adult population. How many times do adults take a day off work every now and then and call in sick when they aren't really sick? Taken a mental health day ? Take extended lunches when the weather gets nicer? What I am trying to say is that as long as we are responsible, "skipping", as either teens or adults, can be a normal part of life. Everyone at some point likes to have time off, away from daily responsibilities.

> *"It's not that some people have will power and some don't. It's that some people are ready to change and others are not."*

> — James Gordon

> *"The first step to getting what you want out of life is this: decide what you want."*

> — Ben Stein

Overwhelmed parents: They say that being a parent is one of the hardest jobs there is. When we become parents, we don't receive handbooks or instruction booklets. The reason parenting can be so challenging is that all children are different, all having their own likes and dislikes, attitudes and types of defiance. Even children from the same family, with the same parents, can have completely different personalities, leaving parents to adapt to their children's separate needs. Add to that different parenting styles, with parents having grown up in completely different households with different rules: one parent believing in one parenting style and the other believing in a complete different form of parenting. It can be very challenging, with both parents thinking they are right and attempting to find a common ground.

~Being a Parent~

It's hard being a parent. As parents, we feel we will forever be responsible for our children. The reason for this is because we become emotionally attached to "being a parent"; we feel that how they turn out is directly related to how we parented them. Not true. Life happens. We can't predict how life is going to go; there are many external factors that occur that we have no control over.

It is true that when they are children, we are fully responsible for the way they act and the things they do, because they are younger and need the direct guidance. However, when they become teens, things change: they become more independent and begin to become responsible for their own actions. It is at this point, when they are spreading their wings, that we have to take a few steps back and let their own individuality come out.

Think back to when you found out you were going to be a parent... we all have these preconceived notions about how we want our kids to turn out. What we are forgetting is that "we" are not "our kids". Although our kids are a product of our creation, they are not 'mini-me's'. They are not exact replicas of ourselves. They have their own minds, their own temperaments and personalities and their own dreams and desires.

When they are young, it is easy to mold our kids into what we want, for we can dress them according to our taste, tell them when it's bedtime, choose their friends and know what they are doing all of the time. Then the fun teenage years begin...

When they become teens, they begin to separate and want to find their own individuality. They want to begin making their own decisions, choosing how they dress, choosing their bedtime, choosing their own friends, etc. This is where and why conflicts begin between parents and teens.

Parents want to stay involved in their teens' lives, and teens want to break away. It's a normal part of growing up. Reassuring to parents is that even though teens are striving for their independence, they still need and want parental involvement; it just has to change. We still need to be there for our teens with guidance and advice, but not in a controlling manner. The role of being a parent changes.

~Parents Blaming Themselves~

Parents sometimes don't understand what happened or where they may have gone wrong. They wonder what has happened to their precious children. They may blame themselves for not doing enough, for working too hard or for not spending enough time with them. Parents may think that had they done things differently – had they not gone through a separation or divorce, had more money or done more things – then things may have turned out differently.

Not true. Don't blame yourself or let your teens blame you for your circumstances or for their behaviour. It is not the traumatic events that your children may have gone through that influenced them negatively; life is full of different experiences, both positive and negative.

Your child will have to learn that life isn't always perfect, that they can't always get what they want and that things will happen that they may not like. It is actually a very valuable life lesson to learn. Problems will arise, it's the way you deal with the circumstances in your life that matter.

Chapter Two

~Acting Out ~

When teens feel mixed up, they can lose control of their emotions quickly and begin acting out. But problems arise when the acting-out behaviours don't satisfy their internal needs, which leads to more acting out and becomes a spiral of emotions.

We all have an internal need to feel cared for, to be loved and to feel secure. It's when these needs aren't met that kids begin to unknowingly internalize their feelings and begin acting out. These feelings turn into negative emotions, thoughts and behaviours that create an "I don't care" attitude. They *do* care; they just put up a guard in order to not feel hurt, to try to make the negative feelings go away. However, the "I don't care" attitude ends up having the opposite effect: it makes things worse and lands them in even more trouble.

That is when you see acting out occur not just at home, but also at school and in the community. Although we may not understand what is affecting our children or teens, and they themselves may not be conscious of it either, they are acting out for a reason. The reason can be anything from biological changes, feeling the stress that may be within the family, or not understanding something at school. It doesn't take much for kids to act out. If they are having problems at school, it may be easier for them to act up and get into trouble than to face the actual problem. In their eyes, if they get sent down to the office, they've dodged the problem because now they don't have to do the work. What they don't see is that it is much easier to get the help when they begin to have problems, instead of ignoring them. By ignoring a problem, it simply becomes bigger and turns into something that will be even harder to fix.

For example: A student who acts up instead of asking for help will just get further behind their peers. Their negative feelings will multiply, and the acting out may become worse. When they see their peers understanding the concept and moving on, their self-esteem will plummet. They may say things like, "I'm just dumb," or "I'm not smart enough."

Instead of verbalizing these feelings, they keep it inside and continue to feel negatively about themselves. What we have to do when acting out occurs is to look at the bigger picture. Try to get inside their heads and be aware of any changes that may have occurred in their life that may be causing the acting-out. It may take some time and be difficult, or it may be an obvious thing, such as a learning disorder or family issues such as frequent arguing within the home.

- Could they be having a hard time in school?

- Do they have problems learning or staying focused?

- Are they being bullied? Are they bullying?

- Could they be jealous of a sibling?

- Has one sibling accomplished something that they haven't?

- Are things okay within the home? Financial troubles? New baby? A move? Divorce?

Remember, kids are very intuitive and pick up on things that we may not even realize, so when trying to find a reason for your child's behaviour, leave no stone unturned. Once you think you know what it could be, then you can work on making changes. Keep in mind that it can be time-consuming; there won't be a light-bulb moment, and you won't find solutions overnight. Their behaviour didn't occur overnight, and solutions won't happen quickly either.

The key is communication, lots of patience and acceptance. Let your kids know that regardless of their actions, you will be there, and try not to say things to them that may make them feel worse. By acknowledging that the acting-out behaviours are happening for a reason, you can work on finding solutions.

I had one student in Grade 1 who appeared very distracted one morning during circle time. I noticed that she was slowly wiping away tears, not wanting to bring attention to herself. I asked her if she was okay, and she replied, "Yes," but was still visibly upset. When I asked her to help me with something, we began talking. It turned out that she was upset because she had witnessed her mom and stepfather having an argument. Kids, especially younger children, don't understand why their parents may fight and assume that any type of arguing is bad. They may be afraid that their parents will get divorced or that one parent may move out.

Sometimes, when we argue with our spouses, we may say things that we don't mean in the heat of the moment, but a child overhearing these things may take them to heart. From an early age, children should be taught that it is okay to have disagreements sometimes and that even though it may be scary to them, they should always be reassured that parental discussions can become heated. Of course, all attempts should be made to keep from fighting in front of kids, but in reality, we don't always make conscious choices or schedule our disagreements for when the kids are not around!

Please remember to debrief with your child after you have had an argument with your spouse, even if you think they didn't hear it. Just touch base with them to make sure they are okay and help them process their thoughts and feelings.

~Losing Control~

Feel like you are losing control? Tired of arguing with your teens? Things can get out of control very quickly, with attitudes and defiance that parents don't like. Arguments begin back and forth, louder and louder, escalating until both parties become frustrated.

What we need to realize is that the more we argue with our teens, the bigger a wall it puts up. We really have be careful of what we are arguing about. The saying "pick your battles" is extremely important when it comes to our teens. Even though some things may drive us crazy, we have to think before we react. Is it really something that is worth arguing about, or will it just make matters worse and create more friction? Maybe choose a time later when you are both in a better space to discuss the smaller issues.

When we don't choose our battles, we get so used to arguing over every little thing that we lose the effectiveness of it. Then, when there is something important to discuss, it doesn't really get heard. If we complain and argue frequently, then they stop listening; they become pros at tuning us out.

~Biological Changes~

Many times, parents get frustrated with their teens for issues that just come with being a teen, biologically. What do I mean by that? Am I saying that just because they are teens and are going through biological changes, it gives them the right to disrespect us and not be accountable for their actions? No, what I am saying is that sometimes the issues we have with teens can be chalked up to hormonal changes.

For example: Many arguments begin first thing in the morning, with repeated attempts to wake up our teens. I'm sure you know how hard it can be just to get them out of bed in the morning. The only thing harder is trying to get them to bed at a decent time! It's biological.

Studies have shown that teens have a different biological clock from that of adults. Even school boards are now looking into having the school day start later, to accommodate teens' different biological needs.

The Toronto School Board is currently experimenting with later start times in selected schools. Classes are starting an hour later (some as late as 10 a.m.), and the results have been very positive. Students report that they like it better, that they feel more rested. They report having more time in the morning to wake up. It has received positive results not only from students but also from staff, who report that the latecomers have dropped dramatically. Previously, students were coming to class thirty to forty-five minutes late, and forty-six percent of Grade 11 students who had first period class were failing.

U.S. studies that are also experimenting with later start times for teens have reported less student depression and fewer dropouts, as well as better test scores and grades. Also due to later start times, enrollment is up. Many students have part-time jobs and work late nights, so for them, a later start time means more sleep. Research is showing that teens' brains are wired to go to bed late and get up late. At puberty, the chemical that induces sleep is secreted around 11 p.m. and shuts off around 8 a.m. Most teens need require eight-and-a-half to nine hours of sleep, most of them not getting close to that due to early start times at school.

What can be done about biological changes? Biological changes affect the teen in different ways, from mood swings to wanting to sleep the day away. Mornings can be frustrating in many households, due to something as simple as trying to wake up your teen. Both your days begin with yelling, frustrations, being late for school and work. Such fun.

The solution? It's a normal process for your teen to want to stay up late and sleep in. Parents need to be creative and find what works best for their teens, but parents also need to realize that all the yelling in the world won't change it.

Mornings are hectic enough without constantly battling with your teens. What parents can do to is to begin to wake up their teens earlier, give them frequent wake-up calls, or maybe turn on their radios or TVs, giving them time to wake up. It's trial and error: try different ways without yelling. No one likes to be woken up in the morning by being yelled at. Remember that our goal is to open the lines of communication. Arguing is not a positive form of communication and often has the opposite effect of its intention. Don't expect them to be rays of sunshine.

~Escalations~

When escalations occur, we as adults have to be able to step back and see that nothing positive will come from this type of interaction with our teens.

Escalations can occur very quickly by one or both parties. Even though our adrenalin may be pumping and we may be absolutely furious with our teens, we have to be the bigger person, label it and end the argument. Tell your teen that you are ending the argument and that they can bring it up again at a later date when you are both in a better space.

Stepping back gives us time to process how and why things escalated and what could have been done differently. Then we can also try to see how things may have looked from their perspectives. Did they feel attacked? As if they weren't being heard? Did we try to enforce our views upon them, without listening to what they had to say? Or were they being completely unreasonable? Knowing when and when not to approach your teen can sometimes make all the difference.

Many factors can create escalations, from headaches to having had a bad day at school or work. It sometimes doesn't take much. Everyone has bad days when the slightest thing can set you off.

Know your teens and know how they handle their frustration and how it escalates. Does it escalate quickly, or does it take some pushing before they reach their limit? Will you have a hole in your wall because you said one thing to them, or do they shut themselves in their rooms? Different people handle frustrations in different ways. It is important to note how you, as well as your teen, escalate.

~Bad Days and Overreacting~

Overreacting happens very easily. I have overreacted many times and said things in the heat of the moment that I have regretted. It's easy to become frustrated; you just want your teen to see things from your point of view! Why won't they just listen to us?! There are days when I come home from work with a headache after a long day at school. (I love working in an elementary school, but some days can be very loud!) I don't want to be grumpy or snap at my kids, so what I do is inform them that it's been a crazy day and that I have a bit of a headache. This usually gives them the heads up to leave me alone for a bit to unwind. It's okay to take space after having a long day.

By sharing your day with them, your kids or your partner, it lets them know that it is not them you are upset with, it is simply the stress of the day. Encourage them to do the same: if they are having a bad day, they should let you know, so that you can give them space. You can talk about it at a later time. It's all about communication and respect.

We have to try to understand where the teen is coming from and what experiences, no matter how big or small, they may have faced or are facing, which may be influencing their behaviour. No matter how trivial the issue may seem to us. Even the smallest issue may have a lasting effect on teens if it is not dealt with.

On top of the stresses that they may be facing, they also can pick up on the stresses that their parents are feeling. No matter how well you may think you are hiding your emotions and stress, they can pick up on it. Remember that our teens are learning from us, just as they did when they were younger. Just because they are now teens, doesn't mean that they have stopped picking things up from us.

When escalations occur, they are watching and learning how we as adults deal with escalating behaviour. There are essentially two ways in which to handle escalations. We can continue the escalation cycle and end up in a bigger mess, or we can step back and regroup. Be real, open and honest with your teens.

Another point is that when you are stressed, you also may unknowingly act differently towards them and have less patience. Be honest with your teens, for they are able to handle more than you think. If you are stressed, in general or at work, talk to them and explain that it has nothing to do with them. Explain that you don't mean to take it out on them.

What parents need to understand is that in talking and being open with your teens about your feelings, it helps them to be open and honest about theirs. It may actually empower them if they feel like they are helping you, thereby teaching them valuable lessons about conflict resolution and empathy. Learning how to resolve conflicts is a valuable lesson to learn in life and can help your teens through many different situations.

What may seem small to you, your teens may perceive as a crisis. If they don't have people they can trust to talk to without the fear of being criticized, they may feel hopeless and take matters into their own hands.

Just look at the teen suicide rate today. Maybe with open communication and a little understanding, we can prevent our teens from taking such drastic measures. Now, keep in mind that I am not saying that we should tell them every little thing that you may have problems with. You don't want to have the opposite effect and stress them out even more. We need to find a fine balance and share stories and emotions with them without telling them everything.

Parents should not strive to be their teens' best friends. They don't need you as a friend, they need you as a parent. They need you to teach them how to act; they need you to teach them structure and balance. What you should be striving for is to find a healthy balance, be there for them and enjoy them, but at the same time, respect that they have their own friends and are developing their own individuality.

Chapter Three

~Friends~

Parents usually take it personally when their teens reach a certain age and want to spend more time with friends. That's normal – exactly what they should be doing! This can be a very trying time for parents, when we don't understand why our kids don't want to spend as much time at home as they used to.

We have to understand and accept that this is a normal part of teen development. They have to find their own individuality and discover who they are. Yes, they may not make the right choices sometimes, but this is all a part of the learning process. Just like you have to learn to crawl before you can walk. Although it's hard, we really have to let them spread their wings and make these discoveries on their own. We can be there to assist and encourage them, but ultimately, it is up to them to find out who they are and what they want from life.

Friends play a vital part of their social development and are often their own support system at times when they don't feel they can approach adults. They feel that only their friends understand them as they are going through the same stages and emotions as they are. This is not always the case, as teens can and do approach adults whom they trust and who they feel will listen to them.

This is why communication is extremely important. We have to learn to listen without passing judgements. If teens are coming to us to discuss something as important as their feelings, then we should acknowledge their feelings and not pass them off as ridiculous or invalid. Who are we to tell them how they should be feeling? We don't always know what they are going through or how challenging being a teen can be. We may think they don't have any stresses, but they do, which is why they often turn to friends who understand them.

When our teens come to us with an issue, we have to listen to them. We have to be careful not provide solutions for them, but rather guide them to talk through the problems and find their own solutions. Teens are very capable and, in time, given the chance, will make proper choices. They just need to feel valued and have you validate their feelings.

While we're on the topic of friends, here's a warning: we have to be careful to not make judgements against their friends based on our own views. We can't say that we don't like their friends because of the way they may dress or based on the amount of piercings or tattoos they may have.

We have to let them choose their own friends and trust that they can surround themselves with good people. Generally, if your teens have a solid foundation and a strong sense of self, they will be able to surround themselves with similar people. If we complain about their friends and try to make them see that they are a bad influence, it may have the opposite effect. You may push your teens further into the friendship as a way to rebel against you.

They may know that the friends aren't the best influence, but having you tell them is not what they need. They need to be the ones to determine that for themselves, in order to separate from the friendships on their own terms.

Reflections: Think of a time when you were younger. Were there any of your friends your parents didn't like? How long were they your friends? How long did it take for you to see that they may not have been the best friend choices?

Allow and trust your teens to see for themselves. How important were your friends when you were a teen? How did it make you feel when your parents complained about your friends? This is when we as parents hope we have laid the proper foundations, teaching them right from wrong. It's these foundations that stay with them, even when they are out with friends that will keep them grounded. It's really not about us, it's about our teens growing up, having fun and learning about life. After all, what we want most for our kids is to raise them to become competent, independent adults.

Many of us didn't know how we were ever going to get through the terrible twos, but we did, as we will also get through the teen years. The magic word for both is patience. Believe me, I know how hard it is to let go and accept that our teens can make the right choices while we sit at home and worry about what they are doing and whom they are with. As I am writing this, my sixteen- and twenty-year-old sons are out with their friends. It is hard, but I have to listen to my own advice and trust in them, trust that I have given them enough guidance that they can distinguish right from wrong.

Friends are vital to your teens' growth. They will be there for them, and your teen will trust them. Your teen will approach a friend with concerns before approaching you. Trust that they can choose the right group of friends.

~The "Not *My* Child!" Syndrome~

As a parent, I completely understand this syndrome. All parents want to believe that their children are incapable of any wrongdoing.

We may be willing to admit that our children were involved in something, but may make statements such as, "Well, he/she was just with those other kids, but my child didn't do anything. My child is only guilty by association." While that may be true, your child still chose to hang around with kids who may not be the best influence. I know how hard it can be; it would just be so much easier if we could just choose whom our teens hang around with, as we did when they were younger. But that isn't how it works! Part of growing up, part of their figuring out who they are and who they want to be, comes from making their own mistakes. When parents overprotect their teens, believing they can do no wrong and even covering up when they *do* make mistakes, that is not teaching them anything. We need to teach our teens to be accountable for their actions.

Sometimes, we need to stop saving them and let them make mistakes, so that they learn how to be responsible and respectful. Let them learn that if they don't respect rules and regulations, then *they* are the ones who will have to face the consequences of their actions.

As a Child and Youth Worker, I see many variations of parenting. While most parents are just trying to do their best, sometimes in attempting to protect and shield our children from society, we inadvertently leave them vulnerable, without appropriate life skills.

One teen had parents who would not allow him to take public transit, trying to shield him from what they may have perceived to be "lower class" people. What if he got on the wrong bus and got lost? What if he missed his stop? What if he met up with people on the bus who harassed him? What if, what if, what if...

Part of growing up, part of raising responsible, well-rounded teens, is to expose them to life experiences. It is only by doing, by trying different things, that we learn. Even something as small as taking public transit or walking to the store. It's part of letting go, teaching your child the skills they need in life to succeed. By teaching your child life skills, we also build their self-esteem.

"The most important thing that parents can teach their children is how to get along without them."

– Frank A. Clark

One year, an elementary student became angry that he was sent down to see the principal. He ended up losing control and began throwing papers from the principal's desk, then hit the pictures off the walls, then pushed the computer onto the floor; he destroyed the principal's office. The police had to be called for assistance to control the child. When his parents were contacted, they blamed the incident on the principal, saying that their son was just upset because he was tired of getting suspended.

While it can be very commendable for parents to want to defend and protect their children, there comes a point when children need to be accountable for their actions, no matter what their age is. Even two-year-olds having temper tantrums can and should be appropriately punished. How else are they going to learn? The student had many difficulties at school, and each time he got into trouble, it was someone else's fault.

We often hear from parents of behavioural students that "they are fine at home." Many times, they are fine at home because there, their parents always meet their tantrums and demands. Sometimes, it is easier for parents to give in to their children than to deal with the repercussions of saying no to them. So when the children come to school, they feel that they can do the same.

~Parental Denial~

Sometimes, it is the parents who are in denial, not wanting to accept that they are having problems with their children. There is nothing wrong with asking for advice or support for your child when needed. It is better to seek help when problems first arise, than to ignore or let things go, in the hope that they will grow out of the stage.

Parenting can be a very difficult job that doesn't come with instructions; there is no manual telling you what to do if you have a problem. We shouldn't be embarrassed or ashamed if we need help dealing with behaviour that comes up. There is no right or wrong way.

Parents with multiple children will tell you that it can vary; a family may have one child who didn't give them any problems and another child in the same family who just didn't respond in the same way and may have caused the family many difficulties.

No matter what your teen is going through, it doesn't give them the right to self-destruct and blame it on what they are going through or what they went through. Yes, they may feel that they have been through a lot, and maybe they have, but that doesn't give them the right to self-destruct. In life, if you have gone through a rough or even traumatic experience, you basically have two choices. One is to dwell on it and use it as an excuse to fail. Or you can learn from what happened and move on.

"We do not see things as they are; we see things as we are."

– The Talmud

This means we often look at things the way we want to see them. If we are down, then we tend to look at things negatively and focus on the past, on the things we cannot change.

Instead, we should make every attempt to see things as they are and put our energy into making improvements, no matter how hard it is. So please don't blame yourself for the way your teen may be acting; everyone reacts differently to situations that occur in life.

It is important to validate the way they are feeling, but also let them know that even though they may be going through rough times, it does not give them the right to mistreat and disrespect the people around them.

"We all have big changes in our lives that are more or less a second chance."

– Harrison Ford

"Only I can change my life; no one can do it for me."

– Carol Burnett

Precautions:

Know their friends: I think that one of the most important things we can do when raising teens is to know their friends. I can't stress enough how important this is.

In knowing their friends, we can know the kind of people that our teens are hanging around and the families they come from, and we can also talk to them and find out a little bit about who they are and what they want from life.

Open-door policy: Take solace in knowing that it's a good sign if your teens are bringing their friends over to hang out. I know it's hard at times, having a house full of teens, but I would much rather have that than have my teen out somewhere where I don't know whom they are with or what they are doing. Having a teen-friendly house provides them with a safe, monitored environment in which to hang out.

If you know their friends, they may take turns hanging out at each other's houses, giving you and the other parents equal opportunities for a break while still knowing that they are safe.

Please note that while it's important to have an open-door policy, it is also important not to invade their space, allowing them to have friends over without constant interruptions.

Negative influences: We have to trust that our teens can choose friends who will not lead them astray. Having said that, there may be times when they do bring home friends who are maybe not the best influence. In that case, we have to allow them to see that for themselves and hope that they see it before it is too late.

Although it is very difficult to sit by and allow them to be around negative influences, again, we have to trust them, as it really is part of their lesson to learn. Now, I'm not saying that there is nothing we can do. We can, of course, talk to them and make them aware of our reasons for not liking their choice of friends. Share your concerns, but it is ultimately up to them to decide whom they hang around with.

A word of caution: forbidding them to hang around a friend whom you dislike may have the opposite effect, because they will still hang around them secretly. If you have given your teens the proper foundation and they have a strong sense of self, they won't be easily led astray.

Believe: Believe in them. Believe that you have done your best and let them open their wings. They will fall, they will mess up from time to time, and that's okay. You don't have to like what they've done or even accept it, but be there and talk them through it. Just because they messed up, it doesn't mean *they* are messed up. Don't give up on your kids.

"The thing always happens that you really believe in; and the belief in a thing makes it happen."

— Frank Lloyd Wright

"If you can imagine it, you can achieve it; if you can dream it, you can become it."

— William Arthur Ward

Chapter Four

-Shutting Down-

When parents become frustrated, teens become defensive and shut down. Even if they're wrong and know it, they are teens and they won't admit it. A stubbornness that sometimes comes with being a teen! Then do you know what happens? Parents become even more frustrated, and escalations continue – things get said in the heat of the moment that usually make things worse, or the parents say things like, "You're grounded." This scenario usually ends up with the teen storming out of the house in a rage.

Who won? No one did. Nothing got resolved, and in fact, it just made matters worse, creating more arguments and issues that you will still have to resolve. Not only do you have to discuss the original problem with your teen, you now also have to deal with the argument that happened because of it. Do you see how easy it is for things to spiral out of control? So this is usually where teens begin to feel frustrated, begin to shut down, communicate less with you and possibly lash out, both verbally and physically.

The culprit is lack of communication. If not resolved, small issues become bigger, until they lead to big blowouts.

The more you argue, the more arguments you create. The more arguments, the wider the gap gets between you and your teen.

~Damaging Words~

Words said during an argument are toxic. Words get thrown around by both parties, but once said, can and do have lasting effects.

Remember the saying: "Sticks and stones can break my bones, but words can never hurt me?" Well, that is not the case. Words can be very damaging and have a lasting effect on your children.

Damaging words stay with your teen. Just because your teen storms out of the house in a rage, it doesn't mean that they haven't listened or don't care. The words may have sank in and become too much.

Teens don't forget about arguments the minute they hit the sidewalk to run away. They don't forget about it when they are with their friends or when they are at school trying to concentrate. They may say they don't care and act like it, but they do. Maybe weeks or months have passed, and you may think they have forgotten, but then, on a day when they are feeling down about themselves, they will think back to an argument when you said something mean to them that you really didn't mean to say. They remember, and now, when they are feeling vulnerable, those words will come back to haunt them. This is a time that teens are most at risk and may turn to drugs and alcohol to numb the pain they are feeling. So just imagine the effect that constant arguing has on your teen.

Damaging words...in younger children: Damaging words also apply to arguments that we may have with our teens or spouses that younger children may overhear. Kids are very perceptive; just because they aren't in the same room when you argue, it doesn't mean that they don't know what is happening and aren't affected by it.

Yes, everyone argues at some point. It can be part of a healthy relationship. But when you do, it's important to touch base with your child afterward. Debrief with them about the things they may have heard and reassure them that things are okay.

~Communication~

Communication with your teen is crucial, and it needs to start before they even become teens. If you have good communication with your teens and can talk about things, they will feel much better about approaching you if anything major does come up. They will also be able to handle things with confidence, as they know they will have the support from family, even if they do mess up sometimes.

Ways to open the lines of communication: Begin building a relationship with your children before they reach the teen years. Do things with your kids; even if you don't have much money, there are always things you can do that cost little or nothing at all. Take them to the park, or go for walks with them and listen to them.

Kids have a lot to say, but sometimes parents are so busy and get caught up in their own issues that we brush them off, which is why so many kids end up in front of the TV and become addicted to video games. I am not saying that TV and video games are bad, but they should be enjoyed in moderation and not used as their only form of entertainment just because you are too busy.

Of course, taking your kids to the park is fine when they are younger. Good luck getting your teen to go to the park with you! However, there are just as many things that you can do with your teen that can strengthen your bond.

You can begin by just talking to them. Talk about a variety of different things. Get their views and inputs on life events. See where their thoughts are going and help them develop their own sense of self. Go camping with them, find a lake, take them fishing or golfing or take them downtown and just walk around for the day. Teach them how to drive. It doesn't really matter what you do with your teen, and it doesn't have to be long and painful. Just spending time with them and taking an interest in them will help strengthen the relationship.

Don't however expect them to want to spend quality time with you every day, just touching base with your teen every once in a while will mean that you are reaching out, reassuring your teen that you care and have not given up.

Case Study:Frustrated One mother became very frustrated with her son's recent behaviour of not listening, showing anger and frustration towards his mother and just generally being what she described as disrespectful. The verbal escalation continued until it escalated into his throwing things off a table in anger. He wasn't intentionally trying to throw something at his mother, but something flew in her direction, and things escalated until the mother physically lashed out at her son. He stormed off, saying that he hated her, leaving her not only frustrated and angry but also feeling like a terrible mother.

Parents everywhere get into heated discussions with their teens that end up with holes punched in walls or harsh words spoken. It's very easy to lose control when our teens make us angry, to say or do things that make us feel like terrible parents.

The important thing to realize is that it is not so much the argument that matters most. What is more important is the debriefing afterward.

After any type of argument with your teen, and after you have both taken time to calm down, always take the time to debrief with them about what happened. It doesn't matter what the argument was about or who was to blame.

Talk about how you are feeling and how you felt about what happened. This takes blame away from them. I'm not saying your teen doesn't have any blame in the incident, but explaining how *you* felt leaves the conversation open for your teen to talk about how *they* felt.

Although the frustrated mother felt terrible, she followed through with her son the next day and discussed what happened. He was open to her conversation, and they could put the incident behind them. The school counsellor has become involved and is providing behaviour strategies and counselling to both the parents and the teen.

If the mother and son were able to effectively communicate then escalating verbal behaviours may have been avoided.

~Anger~

The following story speaks about anger and how words really can be hurtful and have lasting effects.

Nail in the Fence

There was once a little boy who had a bad temper. His father gave him a bag of nails and told him that every time he lost his temper, he had to hammer a nail into the fence.

The first day, the boy drove thirty-seven nails into the fence. Over the next few months, he learned to control his anger, and the number of nails per day gradually decreased.

He discovered that it was easier to control his anger than to drive those nails into the fence. Finally, the day came when he didn't lose his temper at all.

He told his father about it, and the father suggested that the boy now pull out a nail every day that he could control his temper. The days passed, and the young boy finally could tell his father that all the nails were gone.

The father took his son by the hand and led him to the fence. "You have done well, my son," the father said, "but look at all the holes in the fence. The fence will never be the same.

"When you say things in anger, they leave scars just like the holes in the fence. You can put a knife in a man and draw it out, and it won't matter how many times you say you're sorry; the wound is still there. A verbal wound is just as bad as a physical one."

You may think back to things you have told your teen in anger that you now wish you can take back. Words can never be taken back, but new communication, such as saying you're sorry, can always occur. No matter how late it is after they have been said. Even years later, you can talk to your teens and let them know that you are sorry for any hurtful words that may have been said in anger. Your teen may just blow off the apology on the surface, but trust me, it will mean something to them. It is never too late to replace hurtful words with kind ones.

I'm not saying you have to apologize for every argument or unkind word that was said, for only you will know what you are most sorry for. The key is to *mean* the apology.

Remember that apologizing for something doesn't give you the right to be mean anytime and just apologize later. Teens know when you are being real, as opposed to just going through the motions of an apology. You can't fake sincerity. Also don't apologize and then expect them to say they are sorry too. They may, but don't expect it.

~Approaching Your Teen~

A very important part, if not the *most* important part, of approaching your teen to discuss an issue is to never approach your teen when you are upset or angry. I know it can be very hard, and sometimes you are so frustrated with them that you want to tear them apart, but part of being a responsible parent is to restrain yourself sometimes.

Always give yourself time to calm down and process the problem yourself before approaching your teen. This allows you a chance to be in a calmer, non-confrontational state.

If you approach your teen to discuss something when you are angry about a situation, never mind the saying, "an accident waiting to happen". That would be an *explosion* waiting to happen! The approach and manner in which you talk to your teen can make all the difference. It can be a positive experience, or it can make matters worse and lead to more frustrations and a potentially bigger problem.

Opening the door to positive conversations with your teen is the key to getting to know them, to really know how they are doing. When you can openly talk to them, they may begin to trust and open up to you more, knowing that they will not be judged.

Ultimately, you want them to feel that they can approach you about any problem they face, without the fear of being yelled at. Don't be judgemental when your teens do come to talk to you. Allow them to discuss what is bothering them, and don't tell them what to do. Instead, help them through it by allowing them to process it with you. Have them talk about both sides of the issue and the possible outcomes.

Chapter Five

~Empower and Believe~

One of the most important lessons you can teach your kids is to always believe in themselves. Empower them and encourage them to follow their instincts, to listen to the voice inside. Even if their dreams seem impossible or out of reach, believe in them and help them believe in themselves.

Some teens have a purpose, a passion that fuels them. Encourage them to listen to that voice and follow their dreams. However, not everyone knows what they want from life. In that case, just support them and let them know that not knowing what they want is normal.

Have them do some soul-searching. What kinds of things do they like to do? Are they good at a certain subjects? Do they have interests that may lead to a profession one day?

"Nine-tenths of education is encouragement."

– Anatole France

When they are stuck in making a decision, big or small, the best place to find the answer is to look within. One decision will feel like the right one, and the other will make you feel doubtful or uneasy. You can help them in talking things over with them, but ultimately, let them begin to make their own decisions. Stand by your teen regardless of their choices.

> *"A strong positive mental attitude will create more miracles than any wonder drug."*

> — Patricia Neal

~Family Structure~

Today's reality is that we live in a very hectic, fast-paced society that demands more and more from us every day, affecting the family unit.

Whether we realize it or not, family structure over the past few decades has diminished. Life has become so busy that you rarely have time for your family, your spouse or your children. Before you know it, your family is in crisis and no one knows what to do or whom to blame; everyone just blames each other and the marriage, and the family unit falls apart.

There is really no one to blame. Life is busy and hectic, and sometimes, couples just have a hard time working together. Sometimes, all that struggling families need is to step back, take a look at the big picture, see what is happening and realize that things are falling apart because you are allowing life to take over. Sadly, it is sometimes easier to throw in the towel and end the marriage, creating more problems and turmoil for the family.

What people need to realize is that if you don't address what went wrong in the first place, the same mistakes will recur again and again. All of the energy that we are putting out, if not replenished, can lead to many more problems.

~Single Parenting~

Single parenting has become a reality, but it does not mean that your children have to suffer in any way. Sometimes, it is better to end the marriage than to remain in a negative situation.

Some people may think that being a single parent makes things harder and paints a picture of children who are scarred by the added pressures of coming from a single-parent home. Not the case. Yes, it can be a lot more challenging and stressful to the parent, but that doesn't have to have an effect on the children.

In many cases, coming from a single-parent home is better than being brought up in a two-parent home where there is chaos and constant arguing.

Children are smarter than we give them credit for and pick up on what is happening in their home, no matter what the age of the child. It's not okay for parents to assume that the kids aren't affected by their environment or to say that arguments only happen when the kids are not home, are outside or in bed. Kids are able to pick up on the nonverbal cues that parents emit. You may think it doesn't affect them, but it does. They may hide their feelings and keep it inside and may even tell you that they are fine.

~Separation and Divorce~

Using kids as weapons: When a separation occurs, it can be very difficult for all involved. Emotions run wild: anger, jealousy, denial and guilt, to name a few. Then there are financial worries, living arrangements and custody issues which become top-priority.

Whatever the issue with your spouse, it has nothing to do with your children, but they often become the target, the connecting piece, a tool that parents often use unknowingly to get what they want.

Please don't make it about them. By all means, if the marriage isn't working for whatever reason, then separate if things cannot be resolved, but don't use your children as a bargaining tool.

I know that may make some of you defensive, but it is not meant to be an attack against your parenting. I know that you don't want it to be any harder on your children than it has to be, but more often than not, parents bring children into the situation.

Even though we may not be doing it intentionally, we often put our children in the middle. We become so angry at our spouses that we want to hurt them. Some parents think, *What better way to hurt them than to use the kids against them?* If your spouse is driving you crazy and every attempt to work things out has failed, then begin making the arrangements to end the marriage, but don't end being a good parent.

The most important thing to remember is that while you may not enjoy the company of your spouse anymore, your spouse is still your child's parent and always will be. So please don't make your issues with your spouse your child's.
Don't tell your child everything, and don't encourage them to take sides. Work together as parents to let your children know that although you aren't living together anymore, you will both still be there for your child/teen, and regardless of your feelings for each other, you both still love them the same.

If you can relate to these words and realize that you or someone you know has been using their kids as tools, then please at least make an attempt to speak with them. Sometimes, when we are in the middle of a difficult situation, our judgements can be impaired and the parties involved are so frustrated that they may not see the damage they are doing to their kids.

You really should be encouraging your kids to be a part of both parents' lives. They aren't the ones who are separating from the parent, and it is not fair to ask the child to take sides so that you may feel justified.

My hope is for even one person reading this to stop using their child for any type of gain. Please know that I am not judging you. You are not alone in unknowingly bringing your children into your issues; many couples are guilty of this, maybe millions.

Again, open communication with your children or teens. Talk to them about how you may be feeling, but don't force your feelings of hurt and anger onto them. By destroying the relationship that they have with the other parent, you are only creating further conflicts that they have to sort through at a later date and may also alter how they see and interact in their own relationships later in life.

Best-case scenario: Some may say that in any separation or divorce, there is no "best case" scenario. However, when separating or divorcing, there are ways to make things easier for all parties involved.

Sometimes, we have to just step back, remove ourselves from the immediate problem and imagine what the best case would be. What is it that you ultimately want to see? Think about that for a minute. To be able to divide things equally? Civilly? To put differences aside and remain friends for the sake of the children? To co-parent your children efficiently and not try to outdo the other parent?

These things are attainable. I don't think that any of us want to live with the constant turmoil that encompasses a messy separation. If you can't work together to attain this, then it is okay to ask for advice and seek help through mediation counselling. You will be in each other's lives for a long time, so why not attempt to get along for the sake of your child?

Who needs the stress of constantly fighting with your ex? What does it prove? Your kids will grow up seeing who is the parent that is trying to be civil and which parent is the one who continues to cause drama.

Worse-case scenario: Realistically, separations and divorces can be very ugly, leaving parents and kids emotionally and financially drained. It can affect and alter how they see their families. They may not know what their families will look like. With battles occurring between parents, and even battles occurring between the parent and the child, it can be a very confusing time for all involved.

Sometimes, a separation or divorce can completely split up the family, with one parent taking one child and the other parent taking the other child. Think for a second how that may affect your child. Sometimes, it may be necessary to split the family, and that can be okay. The important thing to remember is to try to maintain the relationship between parents and siblings.

A good friend of mine is having a very hard time with his ex-wife. So hard, in fact, that they can't have any civil conversations with each other, unless it is though lawyers. Sadly, this is very common. It happens many times when people separate. If there are no kids involved, then it's no big deal; use the lawyers to divide the property or whatever needs to be negotiated and be done. In that case, you can wash your hands of your ex-spouse and never have to deal with them again.

But if you have children, don't involve them in your troubles. Just because you may not like each other any more, your children still need a relationship with their parent. Don't badmouth each other to your children. You don't need their validation. Your children should be able to love both parents and both families equally, without having to take sides.

Even if parents begin to date other people or remarry, it is in the children's best interests for the parents to remain positive role models in their lives. Do not badmouth your ex's choice of partner.

When separated parents begin to date again, they should continue to place their children's needs above their partners. They say love is blind, but when it comes to choosing a partner, we must always choose ones who will also love and accept our children. While this may seem like an obvious statement, I have seen so many families torn apart because the biological parent becomes so involved with the new spouse that the child feels left out. Every attempt should be made to make the children feel comfortable with the new relationship.

As I've said, children are much smarter than we give them credit for and are able to adjust to different situations, when moving on with your life it is important to show your children that happy, healthy relationships are possible.

Chapter Six

~Respect~

As we've heard before, respect is a two-way street. Period. In order to get respect, you have to earn it. It's pretty simple, actually – you respect people and be real, and you will be treated in much the same manner. I know that many of you may say that you give respect and don't get it in return. That very well may be, but my response to that is to be careful of how you perceive the word "respect".

Respect is not something that you can demand or get just because you are the parent or the adult. Forcing respect will have the opposite effect. You can't demand respect out of force. Any forceful act displays a negative emotion and, in turn, provides a negative reaction.

Once respect is lost, it is much harder to regain. Showing respect is a way of valuing the other person's views. If you don't agree with something your teens do or say, that's okay. Remember that they are their own person and entitled to their own options. You can show disrespect not only verbally, but also in non-verbal manners, and your teens will pick it up very easily. Teens, believe it or not, are experts in knowing who is real and who is not; they know whom they can approach with problems and whom they cannot. They pick up on insincerity. Because respect is hard to get back, you need to clear the air, speak to your teens and explain that what you are both doing right now clearly isn't working, as you are continually fighting.

Talk to your teens and tell them that you want to clear the air and develop better relationships with them. Listen to them, *really* listen to them, and find out what they think the problem is and how they think you can resolve it. Are you being too hard on them? Are they being too hard on you?

Find a common ground and come to a solution together. I'm not saying that a solution will magically appear and that you will no longer have any issues, but by opening up the communication with your teens, you will have begun the process.

Once you begin to get things out in the open, you can slowly work on and rebuild trust. Honesty and respect are always the best policy.

~Pressures~

Today's generation has to deal with many issues very different from those teens did years ago, not only with school and peers but also in facing major changes in single-parent homes. There are many more single-parent homes today than there were years ago. Even when teens do come from a two-parent home, both parents may work full time and therefore don't have much time for their teens. Teens often have to fend for themselves.

Please don't think that I am putting single parents down, for I am a single parent of three kids myself. What I am saying is that there are more pressures and stresses affecting families today. Parents work long hours to provide for their family, spend hours commuting in traffic, have financial worries and, when they do get home, are often exhausted both emotionally and physically.

Understandably, it may be hard to find the energy that our kids not only need but deserve. Is that all we are striving for? Is that the kind of life we want for ourselves and our kids? What message are we sending to our kids? That life is hectic, exhausting and repetitive? When we are not present for our kids, it shows them, maybe not intentionally, that everything else comes first. What's left of us at the end of the day, we give to our kids. We really need to find balance.

~Attitudes~

One of the most important things to learn in life is that a positive attitude can get us through almost anything, no matter how big or small.

The way in which we see the world, the way in which we see the things around us, the way we treat people, all affect our attitude.

You may be wondering why this book doesn't talk solely about teen behaviour, about changing the negative behaviours into positive ones. The answer is simply that there are many different things, attitudes, behaviours, thoughts and feelings that define us that make us who we are.

Who we are reflects how we treat not only ourselves but also the people around us; it also reflects how we treat our teens and has an impact on our relationships with them.

"I am determined to be cheerful and happy in whatever situation I may be, because I have also learned from experience that the greater part of our happiness or misery depends upon our dispositions and not upon our circumstances."

– Martha Washington (1732-1802)

~What Am I Doing Wrong?~

All parents have asked themselves that question at one time or another. Rest assured that you are not alone. Every relationship has its ups and downs, including relationships with our friends, families and spouses as well as relationships with our teens. Ups and downs are a normal part of everyday life. Some days are better than others, while some days are spent wondering how we are ever going to get through them.

I think that the key is to just relax and accept that there is no such thing as a perfect family. By accepting that there will be ups and downs, we will be better able to handle the downs when they do come. As long as the communication is there and expectations aren't too high, you can work through any issues that your family may be facing.

If you are experiencing crisis after crisis and just don't know what to do anymore, know that it is okay to reach out for help.

Start with family and friends. Sometimes, just talking things over, venting and getting another person's point of view is helpful. They may provide you with some ideas that you haven't thought of. If family and friends aren't available, then know that it is okay to seek outside help. You can turn to teachers, your church or outside agencies such as Children's Aid Societies. There are many agencies that offer help to families who are having issues with their children.

You can also call a helpline or speak with someone anonymously. If there are no helplines available, you may also contact your local hospital, and they will provide you with a list of local support numbers.

Please know that asking for help is not a bad thing. You will not be frowned upon or have your kids taken away. All of us at one time or another need help from others. It doesn't make you a bad person or a failure. Asking for help actually has the opposite effect, as it shows that you care and want to find a resolution to your problem.

Never be ashamed to reach out. By letting things go and not seeking help, the problem will just become bigger until it is no longer controllable. The longer we let things go and try to deal with matters independently, the harder they will be to correct.

~Handling Disappointments~

Let's face it, your teens will disappoint you at some point, maybe even at many points, but how you handle these disappointments is vital.

Remember that children and teens learn best by appropriate modelling. If they see you overreact to a situation, that's what they learn. If you overreact to disappointments, it could have a dramatic and lasting effect on your teens – making them feel even worse.

I know it's hard at times to keep your cool in certain situations, but remember that it's okay to step back and end the argument. Tell your teen that you will talk about it later, before things get out of control and things get said that shouldn't. (However, remember to follow through with the conversation later when you have both had a chance to calm down; don't just let it go.)

It's also important to remember that we were not perfect teens either. Accept that mistakes will be made, but don't dwell on them. Deal with them, accept them and move on.

Being able to process and work through conflicts with your teens will strengthen the bond between you. For them, knowing that you will stand behind them through the good times, the bad and the times they screw up will help make them feel safe and secure, giving them a solid foundation. It will also help them develop healthy ways in which to communicate their views.

"When one door of happiness closes, another opens, but often we look so long at the closed door that we do not see the one that has been opened for us."

– Helen Keller

~Forgiveness and Letting Go~

Forgiveness is one of the most important lessons we can learn in life, not only as parents but as people. The ability to forgive someone releases negative emotions and helps us to focus on resolving issues.

Sometimes we have to accept things as they are, realize that mistakes will be made and let go of any negativity we may have in order to move forward.

It's okay to show our teens that we are only human, that we can make mistakes as well. Just because we are grown up doesn't mean that we have all the answers and that we act appropriately in every situation. We can mess up too. Again, it's how we react and how we learn from our mistakes that matter. Don't be too hard on yourself or your teens. We all make mistakes sometimes; the important thing is to accept it, take responsibility for it and move on. Learn from it.

Chapter Seven

~Making Connections~

Connecting with teens can be a very challenging experience. We may want to make connections with our teens, but our teens may be just as happy to keep us away. Teens often don't mean to push us away; they just need and want space.

In attempting to connect with our teens, we may have to deal with a multitude of challenging, potentially explosive, irrational behaviours that may occur without warning and leave us wondering whatever happened to our child. Don't give up; continue to make attempts. Don't take their lashing out personally, even if you are the main target.

Your teens will realize that even though they are doing everything in their power to push you away and break the connection, you are still there for them. That means a lot to them, even if they don't realize it yet.

As I mentioned previously (and will continue mentioning), connections with our teens need to start before they reach the teenage years. The better the relationship with your child in the preteen years, the better the relationship will be during the challenging teen years.

The best way to connect with your children/teens is to do things together and really get to know who they are. Discuss different things with them, and show them that you value their views and opinions.

You may think that it sounds too easy, but by opening the doors of communication with your teens, you are also building connections with them that can last a lifetime. This is a repeat of what I have already written, but it is worth repeating many times.

The best way to connect with your teens is to start connecting with them while they are still young. It is much easier to keep the connection into the teen years if you have built a solid foundation with them when they are young. Communication leads to connection.

~Past~

Don't worry about the past. It is called the past for a reason. There is nothing you can do to bring back past events. Even terrible things that you may have done or said are irreversible. The best way to cure past mistakes is to have learned something from them and to create a brighter future.

Many times, life can become a cycle of events that just seem to repeat. If someone was treated badly when growing up, that may be all they know and they haven't learned how to deal with different situations properly or don't know how to treat people with love and respect.

The world would be a much better place if people would just accept people's differences and treat people with respect. Many times, it is past behaviour or situations that are creating barriers between us and our teens. Although we can't do anything to reverse past events, it's important to note that holding on to it and forever trying to make up for it isn't the answer. By holding on to it, we are, in a sense, keeping it alive and reliving the experience, making it almost impossible to get over.

You may think that your past experience was so terrible that you can't let it go. But whether you grew up in poverty or faced physical or sexual abuse, that was your past. It doesn't have to be your future. By holding onto it, the negatively continues to affect you and your family and can show itself many different ways.

Many amazing people in society have lived through terrible experiences and have gone on to become something better and created the life they wanted, against all odds. No matter what your past circumstances, know that your future and the future of your children depend on you.

> *"Nothing can stop the man with the right mental attitude from achieving his goal; nothing on earth can help the man with the wrong mental attitude."*

– Thomas Jefferson

> *"There is only one person who could ever make you happy, and that person is you."*

– David Burns

~Values and Morals~

From an early age, teach your kids about values and morals. Teach them to care about and respect others, to treat others in the way that they want to be treated. Help them to understand that everyone has differences, be it physical looks, body size or race. Teach them that all of that is just superficial.

We have to help them see above all else that nobody is perfect, that they should be happy with themselves regardless of appearances. What is on the exterior is not what matters, it doesn't define who they are. Who they are is what matters most, and that cannot be seen. Who they are shines through in their personalities, in the way they act. Are they caring towards others? Towards animals? Do they do things for others unselfishly, without wanting things in return?

Those are the kinds of kids we should be trying to raise. How do we instill these values and morals in our kids? That's an easy one. It's not something we have to teach; it's something we have to *be*. By being a person who emits those qualities; by being a kind, compassionate person who always tries to be considerate of others. Kids learn by example. If we want our kids to be kind, considerate people, then we have to show them that behaviour.

There is so much negativity in today's world. Listening to news, all you hear about is violence, disasters and death. Although that may be reality in many parts of the world and even in your city, it doesn't have to be your reality or the reality of your children.

They will hear about the negative things in life, which is why it is also important to show them the other side. Engage your kids and show them that there are also good things out there, good people, people who are willing to help others.

"Be the change you want to see in the world."

– Mahatma Gandhi

You may be wondering why I am talking about appearances and world issues in a book about understanding your teen. But foremost, before they even become teens, we should be working towards raising secure, balanced children who will become teens with a healthy outlook and attitude towards life. Then they will be able to handle the stresses of becoming a teen and maybe not succumb to the negativity of peer pressure, drugs and alcohol.

~Enabling Negative Behaviour~

Starting from an early age, even as early as two, it's very important to begin setting some guidelines for your children's negative behaviour. As we know, around two years old is when temper tantrums begin. If not properly dealt with, these tantrums can continue into the teen years. If you let you toddler get away with something, they learn that all they have to do is cry and they will eventually get what they want.

When they become teens, they can no longer "cry" for something, but instead find other ways, such as guilt trips: "If you loved me, you would..." "Everyone else has one..." "All my friends are going..."

Teens use these manipulations to make parents feel bad. Teens are fully aware of what they are doing; they do what they know will work, and if you have been giving into them since they were little, then why would it change?

They know that guilt trips get them what they want. Even if they know better and know it's wrong, in their eyes, they think it's the parents' fault and, to some degree, they are right. The parents are to blame for giving in to their kids, for enabling their behaviour.

It's hard to "blame" the parents as they often fall into the trap of feeling bad for their teens, of feeling sorry for them. We want what's best for our kids and want them to have what other kids have, but sometimes, overindulging our kids in material things isn't the best way.

Overindulge them in your love and support. For instance, if you have a teen who sleeps in all day, doesn't help out around the house, treats you with disrespect and then, at the end of the day, asks for money or the car keys to go out with friends, that is not okay. The parent is fully enabling their child. We should be teaching our children from an early age:

Respect: If the teens had any respect for the parents, they would not be taking advantage of them.

Responsibility: Also from an early age, kids need to learn about responsibility. If they want something, they have to earn it or work for it.

It's okay to provide your kids with money sometimes, as that is a normal part of the parent/child relationship. However, when your children begin requesting money on a regular basis, then provide them with an allowance and talk to them about budgeting.

When they do become old enough and need more money, then encourage them to get a part-time job. It is never too late to instill these values in your child. You may say that your child has now reached early adulthood and continues to be irresponsible. My bet is that you are still continuing to provide for the teen.

Even if this is the case, it is no too late to begin to put positive changes into place. (Although they may not seem positive in your teens' eyes!)

Talk to your teens about your thoughts and inform them that they have to make some changes. Encourage them to get part-time jobs, so not only can they buy the things they want, but more importantly, it helps them develop a sense of independence and pride and teaches them to be responsible. Don't think that will work? Think your teens will disagree? Are they saying that they have tried to find a job but can't?

Well, if your teens are getting their needs met at home without having to work for it, then why should they get a job? How hard would you look for a job if you didn't have to work and still got the things you wanted ?

Part Two:

Helping parents gain an understanding into their teens' behaviour

Chapter Eight

~At-Risk Youth~

At-risk youth, troubled kids, misfits... society has many different names for kids who suffer from emotional or behavioural issues. Society often labels them as a drain on society, hiding them away in group homes, removing them from regular schools and even placing them in secure treatment facilities. I'm here to tell you that this is not always the case. These kids are still kids that just need understanding, compassion and guidance.

After working in many different group homes, shelters and contained classrooms for behavioural children, I can honestly say that although they may have challenges emotionally or in behaviour, they are just like any other children. They just need to be shown that someone cares. It's human nature; they have basic human needs.

At-risk youth may have come from an environment where nobody taught or showed love and respect to them. Some of these kids didn't have a childhood, but instead had to be the providers.

Many have grown up in households where parents were themselves addicted to drugs or alcohol and exposed their kids to substance abuse from an early age. It's all they know. So is it right for us, for society to brand these kids as useless or a drain on society, or should we be a little bit more compassionate and at least try to make differences in their lives?

These children are looking for a connection to someone who will accept them for who they are – even when they are misbehaving. They don't know or understand why they are acting out; they just know that it gets them into trouble and pushes people away. Many times, it even results in them being removed from their homes.

Although it's extremely challenging at times, they try to push people away in their confusion. They need people who will be there for them, people who will get through the bad times with them, so that they can get to the good.

Often, these kids do want to improve their ways; they are just unsure of how. I strongly believe that with the proper guidance, role models and support, they can turn their lives around and become productive members of society, instead of looking forward to a life of crime and incarceration.

So instead of branding at-risk youth, let's take the time to reteach, retrain and show them by example how to change.

> *"I hear and I forget. I see and I remember. I do and I understand."*
>
> – Chinese Proverb

Inspirational quotations: Many may not value the powerful emotions that come from just reading quotations. They may say that they are only words and that doesn't affect us.

But quotations really can serve as a tool to empower and motivate us. I'm sure that everyone has heard a quotation that resonates with them at some point. They may read a quotation and feel that it is talking straight to them, that it is talking about their situation. Here are a few quotations that I feel are very powerful.

"Human beings, by changing the inner attitudes of their minds, can change the outer aspects of their lives."

– William James (1842-1910)

"Change your thoughts, and you can change your world."

– Norman Vincent Peale (1898-1993)

"An eye for an eye makes the whole world blind."

– Mahatma Gandhi

"Freedom is not worth living if does not include the freedom to make mistakes."

– Mahatma Gandhi

"A friend is a second self."

– Aristotle

"You've got to make a conscious choice every day to shed the old – whatever 'the old' means for you."

– Sarah Ban Breathnack

"We are what we repeatedly do."

– Aristotle

"A strong positive mental attitude will create more miracles than any wonder drug."

– Patricia Neal

~Parents~

A common complaint among parents today is the lack of respect that their teens show towards them. I speak with many parents who are simply frustrated at how their teens speak to them – talking back, not listening and even swearing directly at them. They don't understand why their teens are showing them so much disrespect.

Case Study: One mother called, crying that her sixteen-year-old son had embarrassed her at the laundromat. He wanted money for a scratch ticket to work on while they waited for the laundry.

The mother had said no, as she didn't had much money left and needed it for the laundry. As she related, her son began throwing a fit in the laundry room, in front of others, and said that all he wanted was three dollars for the ticket. Keep in mind that this mother constantly gave her son money. But the son did not let up; he continued to harass his mother. Embarrassed, she gave her son the money to keep him quiet and get him to stop bothering her.

As a prelude to this story, the whole reason they were at the laundromat to begin with is because the son had thrown a fit at home because his laundry had not been done. (There happened to be an extreme heat alert, and with the house already extremely hot, she wanted to wait until nighttime to do the laundry.) Because he wanted clean clothes, he continued to harass her until she went to the laundromat to wash his clothes.

How did she handle the situation? What would you have done differently? Who was to blame? The mother, the son or both? Most important to think about: what is the core, underlying problem within this case scenario?

The underlying issue is that of respect between the mother and son. Of course, as usual, there are a multitude of other issues going on concurrently, although they all come down to the lack of respect. In order for parents and children to resolve any of these issues and have any type of relationship with each other, they need to respect each other. That is not happening here.

So how should that scenario have played out? Well, first of all, at sixteen years of age, if they are capable of complaining about not having clean clothes, then they are also capable of doing their own laundry. Teach your children responsibility.

Secondly, why is a sixteen-year old having a temper tantrum? The answer to that is easy: because it got him exactly what he wanted. In this case, it was clean clothes and a lottery ticket. The mother in this case has to learn to stop reacting to her son's demands.

When parents continue to give in to their teens' demands, they are only reinforcing the negative behaviour. Note: since it took years for this behaviour to develop, it will also take time to undo the demanding behaviour. It will take time and patience.

If my two-year-old granddaughter had a temper tantrum in the store because she wanted a treat, would I cave in and buy it for her? Not a chance. She could scream and cry all she wanted, but it would still not get her the treat. Also, I would not be showing her any type of attention. By ignoring her, I would not be fulfilling any of her attention-seeking behaviour, and she would eventually stop – possibly exhausted from crying, but she would stop!

That is teaching them from an early age that they don't always get what they want. The reason so many kids have temper tantrums is because they have learned that it gets them what they want. If parents ignored the tantrums from an early age, they would eventually stop, and surely would not still be happening at the age of sixteen.

We have all been in stores where kids are having temper tantrums. As frustrating and embarrassing as that can be, the worst part is when you see the parents give in to the crying, just to make their children be quiet and stop the behaviour.

By doing this, you reinforce their behaviour. No matter how much you threaten your children and think it won't happen again, it will.

Only through not getting what they want will their behaviour begin to change. It is when we give in to their tantrums that we reinforce the negative behaviour.

Even though my heart goes out to that mother, she has to learn how to communicate with her son and come up with solutions and expectations that are clear to both parties.

The reason she called me is so that I could talk to her son for her. That creates yet another issue, as the mother has to learn to effectively communicate her feelings to her son. I can't make him respect her; only she can do that by talking to him. They need to learn to communicate with each other without disrespecting each other.

Her complaint is that she gives and gives to him but does not get the respect back that she wants. That is because you don't get respect by providing material possessions – by buying them cell phones, or multimedia equipment or by handing them money every time they leave the house.

When parents do that, the child learns to expect these things, and when the parents say no to some requests, they have tantrums and still end up getting what they want. It becomes a cycle. A cycle that ends up leaving the parents frustrated and out of control. We have to teach them that negative actions don't get positive results.

My advice for Mom: As frustrating as it can be, it is not too late to change the behaviour. I'm not saying it will be easy, as new behaviours, a new way of communicating with your son, may be hard at first and may even get worse before it gets better, especially when he finds out that he won't be getting things handed to him whenever he wants.

Eventually, you will both begin to see that respect is a two-way street. It is about give and take; it's about balance. Some issues will require more negotiations than others, but that's okay. The key is to be consistent with your actions. It can be difficult to begin the process without causing further tension. The mother may not be sure how to begin, and the son may not be willing to listen or abide by the new set of rules. (Especially if the new rules affect his current behaviour!)

Don't think that you are being mean by not giving and giving to your children. They need to know that things in life won't be handed to them. If they want something, especially at sixteen, they need to learn responsibility, and yes, that includes being responsible for their own actions.

From one teen's point of view, his mother doesn't understand him and doesn't trust him. This creates a problem, as the more that he complains and doesn't listen to his mom, the more they argue.

What he needs to understand is that it is not just his mom's fault, he also needs to take responsibility for his own actions, which are creating the friction. His mom may ask him a simple thing, and it is his reaction by blowing up that leads to swearing and being disrespectful towards his mom that fuels the battles.

If he has a problem with how his mother is treating him, then he has to find a manner in which to verbalize it to her. If he wants her to treat him with respect and understanding, then he has to treat her that way too.

They need to find a common ground and stop blaming each other. When teens feel that parents are too controlling, they begin to pull away. Some parents want to be in complete control of their teens, especially their daughters, understandably. But the over-protectiveness can have the opposite effect and push them even further away.

The best thing we can do is to sit our teens down and voice our concerns constructively. We must explain to them why we may be concerned and give them a chance to respond, without interrupting with negative remarks.

We must provide the chance for them to come up with some options and let them decide what they think should be done, what they think the proper action should be and, if it fails, what the appropriate punishment should be.

By allowing them to be a part of the solution, you are showing them that you value and trust their input.

~Curfews~

A common argument between teens and parents is curfews. Parents feel that curfews are set in place to give the child boundaries, and teens think that curfews are made to be broken! They feel that curfews are too controlling.

Curfews are a touchy subject, as there are many different views on it. Some parents are very strict and set a specific time limit, while other parents set the curfew based on what the teen is doing. Either way, the common denominator is communication with and trusting in your teens.

Some say that curfews are an essential part of learning responsibility. While this can be true, I think that the most important part of setting curfews is making the teens a part of it. Work together to set a reasonable curfew based on what they are doing. It is the parents who involve their teen in the decision who usually don't have to worry about them breaking curfew.

Parents who are too strict, who are unrealistic or who don't have good relationships with their teens are often the ones who complain about their teens not coming home on time. This causes further arguments. Teens aren't against curfews; they just want them to be reasonable.

~Breaking Curfew~

A common mistake that parents make when their teens do come home late is to question them right away about where they were and what they were doing. It doesn't really matter. Well, it does, but all you need to know in that instant is that they are home, safe.

Let them know that you will be talking about it tomorrow, that there will be consequences, and let them go to bed. Questioning them right away will only lead to an argument, as you have been sitting up, waiting to pounce on them for breaking curfew. Try leaving it until the next day when you can both talk about it calmly.

Again, involve them and ask them what they think a good consequence should be: an early curfew next time, extra chores around the house or maybe not going out next time. It really depends on the situation; each situation may differ. Some will test the theory and break the curfew to see what the consequence, if any, will be.

~Safety ~

Keeping our teens safe is always in the forefront of our minds whenever they go out. I can't stress enough the importance of instilling in your teens that, while out with their friends, if they become involved in any unsafe situations, they should call home.

You should have a conversation with your teens as soon as they begin to become more social. You should let them know that they can always call home if they feel unsafe or cannot drive, for whatever reason, whatever the time.

Some parents have even created a password that their teens can use when calling home, in case they become involved in a bad situation. The password lets the parents know that they need to be picked up for safety reasons. They also need to be aware that if they do call to be removed from a bad situation, that they will not face any punishment for calling, no questions asked, at least not right away.

The next day, you can try to talk to your teens about what happened the previous night, but if they don't want to talk about it, reassure them that you are there to talk if they need to and let them know that they made the right decision to call home for support.

They may or may not want to talk about it; the important thing to note is that in calling, they made a responsible decision.

One of the mothers that I have counselled stated that she locks the door at a certain time if her child is not home, thinking that it will teach him a lesson.

How safe is that? Her child then has to spend the night outside, in potential danger, to fend for himself.

Home should always be a safe place for the children, regardless of the issues you are having with them.

For the most part, teens do feel as if they fit into their environment, but sometimes, they feel that it can depend on their appearance.

They feel that if they look, dress or act in a manner that is not "the norm", then people in society often make judgements and don't want to interact with them, often not even giving them a chance. Teens sometimes do dress in extreme ways, but many times, it is because they feel different and feel as if no one cares, so they begin to rebel.

Sadly, the rebellious children often push parents and people in society further out of their lives, instead of trying to gain acceptance. Then it becomes harder for the teens to feel like a valued member of society.

Of course, not all teens feel that way. Many are secure and can dress and act the way they feel is right and don't care what peers or society feel. We, as a society, really do need to stop placing judgements on teens and make every attempt to get to know them, regardless of their appearance.

Chapter Nine

~Teenage Pregnancy~

Teenage pregnancies happen. They happen all over the world, no matter what our socioeconomic status is or what your religion is. They happen, even if you think that it won't happen to your teen, even if your teen is taking precautions. They happen. Please don't automatically think that just because your teen is on birth control that they will not get pregnant, and don't assume that they were acting irresponsibly.

Teens who become pregnant are often in disbelief, are scared, are unsure of what to do and don't know where to turn for help. They are facing a lot of physical as well as emotional changes.

"I'm having a baby…"

When you find out that your teen is having a baby, please be aware of your reactions. It can be a very difficult time for your teens, and telling their parents is one of the scariest times for them. They are very afraid of parent reactions: will they get kicked out of the house? Will they be disappointed? Will their parents force them to have an abortion or give up the baby?

Parental support, when finding out that our teen is pregnant is one of the most important things that we can do to help our teen through one of the toughest times of their life. They, now, more than ever need to know that we are there for them and will help them through.

The amount of support that your teens have can make all the difference in the outcome of your teens' pregnancy.

If your teens have your full support and you are willing to help your teens through their pregnancy and with the baby, then it can be a wonderful experience. A new baby, although a lot of work, also has many rewards. On the other hand, if your children have to face their pregnancy alone without the blessings and support of their family, then it will be a difficult time for your teens and can have lasting dramatic effects upon both the teens and their babies.

Abortion can also have lifelong emotional effects, depending on how your teens look at the situation. Whose decision is it? When a teenage girl gets pregnant, it is ultimately up to her what to do about the pregnancy, as it is her body. The partner should be there to help her make the decision and to offer his input, but ultimately, it is up to her. He will have to support her decision in the end.

Although it may be hard for a teen to raise a baby, it can be done. There are lots of support services out there for teenage parents to access; all they need to do is ask for the help. It is great if their families are supportive, but there are many community support services that teens can use.

What they need: A pregnant teen requires support, reassurance, more support and more reassurance.

Support: All teens need to feel supported, especially pregnant teens. They need to feel that no matter what they decide to do, they will be supported in their decisions.

Reassurance: Because this can be one of the scariest times for your teens, they need to feel reassured. They need to have their parents/guardians reassure them that everything will be okay, regardless of their decisions.

Education: Pregnant teens' need to be educated in the options that are available. Basically, your teen has three choices: to have the baby, to have the baby and put it up for adoption or to terminate the pregnancy.

Teens need to weigh upon each decision, as there can be pros and cons to each option. Again, they need to look at emotional factors as well as realistic expectations.

~Suicide~

Suicide is tragic, especially when in occurs with teens who have not yet really started their life. Teens who commit suicide think that there is permanence to whatever issues they are facing. They tend to look at only their present situations and feel that there is no way out.

Teens who attempt or commit suicide feel that no one cares and that nothing anyone says or does will make a difference. They feel as if no one will miss them when they are "gone". Sadly, it is the ones who are left behind that are left to deal with all the emotions; the blame and all the what-ifs.

What we have to remember is that it was ultimately their choice, for whatever reason. So often, the people closest look for someone to blame.

Many times, teens end their lives over breakups. Sometimes, it is easier for the parents of teens who have committed suicide to blame the ex-boy- or girlfriends or the group of friends that they were hanging around.

It could have been one of many different reasons. What we have to remember is that it was their choice in the end. Each of us is solely responsible for our own actions and decisions, good or bad. The best way to honour someone who has committed suicide is to remember them, the good times, and to move on with your life.

~Youth Suicide~

Statistics: Warning signs and risk factors

Suicidal tendencies don't just appear out of the blue: people usually display a number of warning signs when things seem so wrong in their lives that they've simply given up hope. Because adolescence is such a turbulent time, it may be difficult to distinguish the signs that lead to suicide from the changing, sometimes uncertain, but otherwise normal behaviour of teens.

Behaviour changes to watch for:

– withdrawal from family and peers
– loss of interest in previously pleasurable activities
– difficulty concentrating on schoolwork
– neglect of personal appearance
– obvious changes in personality
– sadness and hopelessness
– changes in eating patterns
– such as sudden weight loss or gain
– changes in sleep patterns
– general lethargy or lack of energy
– symptoms of clinical depression

Though many suicidal teens appear depressed or downcast, others hide their problems underneath a disguise of excess energy. If an adolescent starts displaying uncharacteristic agitation and hyperactivity, it may also be a signal of an underlying problem. This restlessness may take the form of confrontational or aggressive behaviour.

More obvious signs that an adolescent may be suicidal include low self-esteem and self-deprecating remarks. Some teens come right out and talk or write about their suicidal thoughts; this should be taken seriously, not ignored with the hope that it's a passing phase. Any previous attempts at suicide are loud and clear cries for help, which demand responses before it's too late.

Causes of adolescent suicide: Many troubling and difficult situations can make a teen consider suicide. The same emotional states that make adults vulnerable to considering suicide also apply to adolescents. Those with good support networks (e.g., among family and peers, or extracurricular sport, social or religious associations) are likely to have an outlet to help them deal with their feelings.

Others without such networks are more susceptible during their emotional changes and may feel that they're all alone in times of trouble.

Apart from the normal pressures of teen life, specific circumstances can contribute to an adolescent's consideration of suicide. It's especially difficult when adolescents are confronted with problems that are out of their control, such as: divorce, physical or sexual abuse, emotional neglect, exposure to domestic violence, alcoholism in the home, or substance abuse. About 80% of suicides are committed by people who are depressed.

Depression is a mental-health disorder; it causes chemical imbalances in the brain, which can lead to despondency, lethargy or general apathy towards life. Almost half of fourteen- and fifteen-year-olds have reported feeling some symptoms of depression, which makes coping with the extensive stresses of adolescence all the more difficult.

Symptoms of depression in youth are often overlooked or passed off as being typical "adolescent turmoil". Another serious problem that can lead teens to suicide – or aid in their plans to end their lives – is the easy access many of them have to firearms, drugs, alcohol and motor vehicles.

For the general population, about 30% of suicides involve firearms; of all firearm-related deaths that occur, more than half are suicides. (Source: Canada.com, © 1996-2009)

Teenage Depression and Suicide – The Facts

Teenage suicide is a Canadian epidemic that we need to take seriously.

– Suicide is the second-leading cause of death for teens in Canada and the third-leading cause of death in the U.S.

– Suicide and attempted suicide have increased 300% in the last thirty years.

– Teen/youth suicide rates have tripled since 1970.

– Nine out of ten suicides take place in the home.

– For every completed suicide, there are an estimated thirty to fifty attempts. Seventy percent of suicides occur within the hours of 3 p.m. to midnight (when they could be saved).

– Males complete suicide four times more often than females do. Females account for 75% of the attempted suicides (mainly with drug overdoses).

– Approximately one-third of teens who die by suicide have made a previous suicide attempt.

– Males tend to use more violent means, e.g., guns, hanging.

– Only 33 to 50% were identified by their doctors as having a mental illness at the time of their death, and only 15% of suicide victims were in treatment at the time of their death.

– An estimated 80% of those who commit suicide give some warning of their intentions or mention their feelings to a friend or family member.

In 1996, more teenagers and young adults died of suicide than from cancer, heart disease, AIDS, birth defects, strokes, pneumonia, influenza and chronic lung disease combined. From 1980 to 1996, the rate of suicide among African American males aged between fifteen and nineteen years increased by 105%.

For every two homicides in the U.S., there are three suicides.

Having a firearm in the home greatly increases the risk of youth suicide.

Sixty-four percent of suicide victims between ten and twenty-four years old use a firearm to complete the act.

Due to the stigma associated with suicide, available statistics may well underestimate the problem.

~Cutters & Control~

Teens sometimes feel so much internal turmoil that they begin to cut themselves as a way of escaping their feelings. Cutting themselves, bleeding, in their eyes allows some negative/hurt feelings out. To them the blood represents the hurt feelings leaving their body. Cutting therefore releases some of the pressure they feel and temporarily makes them feel better.

When teens are under a lot of stress and are unable to control their feelings, don't know how to express how they are feeling or don't have anyone to turn too they become overwhelmed. The overwhelmed feelings, if not dealt with, continue to build in their body. The act of cutting not only provides a physical release for them but it is also about control, cutting themselves is something only they can control. Cutters are mostly female, however many males also cut, both sexes are very good at concealing their cuts. Most cut on wrists or arms but some of the more serious cutters will cut where it can be easily concealed.

The dangers of cutting.....

Once teens begin to cut, depending on the severity of their inner turmoil, it can be a very hard process for them to stop. If they don't receive help in dealing with their emotions, they will continue to mount and the teen will continue to feel the need to cut. In their eyes, a form of self medicating. They will do anything to cut, and at times feel a 'physical need' to cut.

Don't confuse cutters with teens who are suicidal, for it is a completely different situation. While suicidal teens want to die, cutters don't want to die, they just want the hurt feelings inside their body to go away. One client I worked with had such extensive damage to her whole body, that skin was barely visible, it was scar tissue upon scar tissue, becoming so good at cutting that she was able to carve in between the veins in her wrists, arms and legs. The physical need to cut at times is so strong that I have seen clients break light bulbs to use as a tool to cut. Extensive hospitalization is required in those instances and any item that may be used to cut needs to be removed from access.

Who is at risk of cutting......

Please don't assume that it is only troubled youth who resort to cutting, for I have seen many teens who come from stable, loving homes who have attempted cutting as means of dealing with their mixed emotional state. Teens who feel like they have no control over their own life, parents who wish to control every aspect of their teens life in attempts of helping their teen, in retrospect can do more harm than good. Teens need to feel like they have some control over their life. It is when teens feel stuck, like they have no control over their own life that they 'take' the control into their own hands, as a way of saying "this I can control". If this is the case, work with your teen, listen to their concerns, accept their input and come up with agreed upon solutions. Touch base often with your teen, learn to talk openly about how they are feeling, what they want, by doing so you will open up the lines of communication allowing your teen to feel heard. The earlier you are able to get help for a teen who cuts the easier it is to treat. Outside intervention, such as counselling is also recommended to allow your teen the opportunity to talk about how they are feeling to a trusted adult. Family counselling would also benefit and provide you with ways to deal with and accept any concerns.

~Losing Hope: The effects of drugs, alcohol and depression~

It is when teens lose hope in themselves that they begin to look for other things to make them feel "happier". This is when they can succumb to negative peer pressure and begin to consume drugs and alcohol to ease their confusion and feelings of worthlessness.

The drugs and alcohol temporarily make them feel better, but many teens already feel invincible, so with the added effects of drugs, alcohol and peer pressure, they often wind up making bad choices and going down the wrong path. It is not too late at this point to help them, but how you approach and deal with a teen on the wrong path is crucial.

They can be very defensive, as their perception becomes distorted. They may believe that since they feel better when they are under the influence, that it can't be bad; they can almost defend their use as therapeutic. It is therefore not in the parents' best interest to come down hard on the teens, for that will only push them further away.

Often, the teens are fully aware that what they are doing is not okay, but they somehow feel empowered and gain a false sense of security from the effects of the drugs and/or alcohol. How quickly you can help your addicted teens depends on many factors: the length of time they have been using, what they have been using and the events that are occurring in their lives. You may be wondering what the events are that can be affecting their use. Things such as peer pressure, their school life, how things are at home and how they feel about themselves, to name a few.

When teens begin to use daily, it can be a sign that they aren't feeling strong inside, that they aren't getting the inner satisfaction from their current situation. Many times, low self-esteem is the cause of drug and alcohol use. Ask yourself: Are there problems in the home? Do your teens feel as if they have no one to talk to? What are the relationships like within the home, and what kinds of peer relationships do they have? Could there be mental-health concerns, such as depression? Have you noticed a change in their moods, friends or grades in school? If you have noticed any sudden changes in your teens' temperament and all attempts to reach them have failed, it may be time to approach your doctor or school counsellor.

Sometimes, teens approach their parents and state that they are feeling depressed, only to have the parents dismiss their concerns as silly or not valid, but who are we to determine how our teens feel? Parents often don't want to admit it, as a teen who suffers from depression may put a negative label on the family. Too many people perceive depression as a weakness, but when properly diagnosed and treated, depression is easily controlled and doesn't have to be a life-long sentence.

When you begin to have problems with your teens, you really need to look at the big picture, step outside of the circle and try to see how they may be feeling. This is why I am trying to emphasize that open communication with your teens is essential, because when your teens feel that they are a part of the family unit and feel valued and listened to, they feel as if they can approach their parents with anything. Then they can begin to build a strong sense of self and obtain the power, strength and courage it takes to make positive choices, instead of turning to drugs and alcohol as a way of escaping their feelings.

Keep in mind that most teens at some point do experiment with alcohol. Just because your teens have been drinking doesn't mean that they have a problem with alcohol. It is when they feel the need to drink to have fun and think they can't have fun without it that it becomes a problem.

Can teen substance use and abuse be prevented?
Talking openly and honestly with your teens and keeping a healthy home life may prevent your teens from trying alcohol and drugs.

You can help prevent substance use by using these tips:
– Talk to your children early about what you expect in their behaviour towards alcohol, tobacco and other drugs.

– If your teens think that you will allow substance use, they are more likely to try drugs or alcohol.

– Keep your teens busy with meaningful activities, such as sports, church programs or other groups.

– Expect your teens to follow the household rules. Set reasonable penalties for bad behaviour and consistently carry them out.

– Keep talking with your teens. Praise your teens for even the little things they do well.

– Know your children's friends. Having friends who avoid cigarettes, alcohol and drugs may be your teens' best protection from substance abuse.

What is teen substance abuse? Many teens try alcohol, tobacco or drugs, but using these substances is not safe or legal. Some teens try these substances only a few times and stop. Others can't control their urges or cravings for them. This is substance abuse.

Teens may try a number of substances, including cigarettes, alcohol, household chemicals (inhalants), prescription and over-the-counter medicines and illegal drugs. Marijuana is the illegal drug that teens in Canada use most often, with about one in three high school students using tobacco and marijuana.

Illicit teen drug use as of 2003:
* 8th grade – 30.3%
* 10th grade – 44.9%
* 12th grade – 52.8%

Part 2: From the teens' point of view: What teens think...
"I don't care."

"You don't care."

"Why do I have to listen to you?"

"You don't understand."

"Whatever."

Chapter Ten

~How Teens Feel~

When I first decided to write a book about teen behaviour, I felt the need to incorporate the thoughts and feelings of teens themselves. In order to fully understand them, we really need input from them about where they stand and how they feel about different issues.

How do they feel they fit into their environment? How do they get along with the people in their lives? Family? Friends? Do they feel they are treated differently just because they are teens? Thoughts about schooling? What pressures do they feel they face? What do they think about drug and alcohol use? Do they feel things are different or harder than they were generations ago? If they don't have good relationships at home, where do they think things began to go wrong? What are some of the changes they would like to see? What kind of relationships do they have with their parents? Siblings? What changes, if any, would they like to see within their family? Do they feel they can approach their parents? If parents are divorced, how has that affected them? What kinds of stresses do they feel? What do they want from the future?

These are some of the questions that teens face daily. It can be a lot to take in and deal with. This is why it is important to open up communication with our teens. They don't need any more problems that the ones they are facing by just being in the teenage years. The main complaint from teens that is that their parents don't understand them and don't trust them; they feel that their parents are unapproachable.

Think back for a minute to when you were a teen. What kind of relationship did you have with your parents? Did you feel that they understood you? Did you feel that you could approach them when something was bothering you? Were you completely open and honest with them? About everything?

So you see, the complaint from teens that parents don't understand them, that parents are unapproachable, is normal. It's a normal process for your teen to pull away, as they strive for their independence and try to find themselves. They don't want you telling them who they should be. They don't want you to know everything they are doing. It may scare you, and you may say that they are your children and you think that you have every right to know what they are doing.

In most areas, once children reach sixteen years of age, they are considered adults and therefore can make decisions on their own. I know that many of you may be laughing and are saying that your teens cannot make important decisions on their own. Maybe they can and maybe they can't; maybe they won't always make the best decisions, but it is their lesson to learn. It is by making mistakes along the way that we learn and grow.

-Letting Go, Spreading Wings-

When my daughter was seventeen, I let her live in a different province for several months, with a friend's family. We were moving between provinces in the middle of the school year, and she wanted to stay and finish off the school year there.

Listening to my own advice was hard; it felt funny not having her around, and our family unit changed. But as hard as it was, I had to trust and have faith in her.

For six months, she lived in a different province and, throughout that time, even moved into an apartment with another friend, which was even harder for me to accept. I worried about how she was eating, how she would wake up in the morning for school and, of course, her having complete freedom and still continuing to go to school every day.

Of course, I gave her a wake-up call every day, to make sure she was up and ready for school, but aside from that, the rest was up to her. She got herself to school and to her part-time job, grocery-shopped, cooked for herself (with a few calls home for instructions), kept up with school work and graduated. I could have said no and forced her to move provinces with us, but doing that would have meant that I didn't trust her and didn't have faith in her, which I did. It all comes down to having open lines of communication with your teens.

I'm sure she didn't tell me everything, but she could live and learn, creating her own independence. Even upon graduating and moving to Ontario, as soon as she could, she moved into her own apartment. Four years later, she is now in her second year of university and is raising a two-year-old daughter independently. There was no magical secret to raising her; I just incorporated all of the advice I have given in Part One: open communication, trust, belief, knowing friends, having an open-door policy (even on days when I just wanted peace), listening without enforcing my own views and choosing battles.

So even though it may scare you that the legal age is sixteen, know that it is possible for our teens to make informed decisions regarding their own lives. Start as early as you can to develop a bond with your child; be approachable and don't judge.

~Teen Complaints and Feedback~

Undoubtedly, the main complaint from teens is that they feel misunderstood; they feel that their parents always tell them what to do, that their parents always think they are right and just don't trust them. Some teens who do have good relationships with their parents report that their parents take the time to talk to them and listen to what they have to say.

The parents allow their teens to speak their mind, show trust and have open discussions with their teens without telling them what to do. Teens who have this type of relationship with their parents feel trusted and valued and are more likely to open up to their parents, because they feel like what they have to say matters.

~Last Words of Inspiration~

Don't take life too seriously! Don't strive to be the perfect mother, father or family... there is none. Just enjoy the time that you have, even the hectic and crazy days. Before you know it, they will be grown up and you will wonder where the time went.

Take a few minutes to think: What is it that you want them to remember about their childhood? What memories are you instilling in them? What are some of the memories that you have from your childhood?

Appreciate. Learn to appreciate all of the different stages that your children go through, for each state has its fun times as well as its challenges. Face the challenges. Don't get annoyed at the challenges you face with your teens; no teen is perfect, and each one is unique. Accept the challenges and learn something from each obstacle you face.

Don't raise your kids with blinders on. Don't think that just because you don't talk about or expose them to such things as drugs, alcohol or sex talks that it doesn't happen. The best thing you can do for your teens is to be realistic. Talk about the issues they may face, and educate them as to what can be done if they face certain issues. Let them know that you will be there for them, even if they may not always make the right decisions. Life is a learning process; we as well as our teens need to learn from the mistakes that we make.

Don't be too judgemental or overbearing. Let them know that you care without being too controlling. Take care of yourself, so that you can take care of those you love. Laugh often; try every day to bring a little laughter into your teen's world.

Our children are our biggest legacy....Don't Give Up On Your Teens.